Cynthia Gibson

A Botanical Touch

DECORATION · GARDENS · PARTIES

With Susan Carlton & Coco Myers

Photographs by William P. Steele & Matthew Mattiello

Design by Julio Vega

VIKING STUDIO BOOKS

VIKING STUDIO BOOKS
Published by the Penguin Group
Penguin Books USA Inc., 375 Hudson Street, New York, New York 10014, U.S.A.
Penguin Books Ltd, 27 Wrights Lane, London W8 5TZ, England
Penguin Books Australia Ltd, Ringwood, Victoria, Australia
Penguin Books Canada Ltd, 10 Alcorn Avenue, Toronto, Ontario, Canada M4V 3B2
Penguin Books (N.Z.) Ltd, 182–190 Wairau Road, Auckland 10, New Zealand

Penguin Books Ltd, Registered Offices: Harmondsworth, Middlesex, England

First published in 1993 by Viking Penguin, a division of Penguin Books USA Inc.

1 3 5 7 9 10 8 6 4 2

Library of Congress Cataloging-in-Publication Data
Gibson, Cynthia.
A botanical touch: decoration, gardens, parties / Cynthia Gibson;
text by Susan Carlton and Coco Myers;
photographs by William P. Steele and Matthew F.-G. Mattiello.
p. cm.
ISBN 0-670-84292-3
1. Flower arrangement. 2. Gardening. 3. Gardens. 4. Entertaining.
I. Carlton, Susan. II. Myers, Coco.
III. Title.
SB449.G5 1993
793.2—dc20
92-36160

Printed in Hong Kong
Set in Caslon 540
Designed by Julio Vega

For my mother,
whose grace, sense of fairness,
and limitless love
created the world in which I live

Acknowledgments

I am very grateful for the opportunity I had to work with a team of outstanding people who without hesitation gave their talent and expertise to make my vision a reality.

I would like to thank Bill Steele for his unerring eye, his patience, and perfect photographs; Susan Carlton and Coco Myers for their diligence, ability to translate my thoughts, contend with horticultural language, and smile throughout the process; Julio Vega, for his brilliant design, attention to detail, and genius; Becky Linney, who shared family recipes, gathered flowers, vines, and branches, and ran endless errands—without her help, I would not have been able to style the photographs; and Lynn Eaton, who helped research and identify the most obscure plants and topics.

I thank the people at Viking Studio Books for their commitment and enthusiasm, especially Michael Fragnito and Barbara Williams for their confidence and trust in my concept; my editor, Martha Schueneman, for whom I have great respect and whose dedication was invaluable; and Roni Axelrod, who oversaw production and whose knowledge ensured a beautiful book.

Nancy Love, my agent, provided excellent counsel; I thank her for bringing us all together.

I salute you all for your sense of humor and professionalism.

The following colleagues, friends, and family opened their hearts, doors, and garden gates: Shelley Atwood, Louise Baker, Liller Biewend, Romayne Bockstoce, Debi Camarota, Lynn Chase, Francesco and Frances Corrias, Carol and Joseph Donnelly, Jean Eaton, Carol Hollingsworth, Marion Hosmer, Pat Jester, Pat Linden, Shanlee Linney, Matthew Mattiello, Cynthia Maxim, Nancy and Alan Raynes, Ann Spoor, and Suzy Verrier.

My husband, James Gibson, once said to me, "If you speak from your heart, all will listen and remember." It is my hope that I have honored his words, love, and patience in this book. I cannot thank him enough.

Contents

Introduction

I remember picking my very first flowers at the age of four from a garden that belonged to a friend of my grandmother's. The brilliantly colored zinnias were irresistible. My hand found its way through the narrowly slatted fence to retrieve one of the zinnias, as well as a few poppies and other carefully tended blossoms. Upon presentation of my bouquet to my mother, I was informed of my trespass, and quickly learned the art of the formal apology. But my love of flowers was not forsaken. I was presented with a tiny corner of earth to plant my very own flowers and vegetables. Since then, I've almost never been without a garden.

For me, flowers as well as other types of botanicals—fruits and vegetables, leaves and vines—pervade almost every aspect of design. Botanicals inspire the way I decorate a room, envision a garden, or set a table.

As a watercolorist and designer of floral textiles and home furnishings, I look at botanicals as decorative images, which is actually how they've been treated by many artists and artisans over the centuries. The reverence for nature appears in all sorts of guises, some more subtle than others—from garden scenes in a muted Oriental rug to carved pineapple finials on a nineteenth-century English bed. Botanical motifs continue to look fresh in patterns on wallpaper, fabrics, linens, china, needlepoint pillows, and rugs. There is an unending supply of inspiration to be found in nature, with countless modes of interpretation. Far from being a one-note style of decoration, botanical motifs encompass a broad range of styles and sensibilities. A print of small blue and white bachelor's buttons has a sweetness and guile, while a pattern of large parrot tulips has a strength and exoticness.

The notion of design can be extended to the garden itself. When I look at a landscape, I see more than earth and plants: I see an opportunity to make an aesthetic statement with color and texture. People garden partly because they want to create something from the ground up, but also because they want to enhance their surroundings. Successful gardens—flower or vegetable—have been orchestrated with an eye to an overall effect. Even a simple herb garden can be planned in a painterly way.

I could not love gardening as I do without having it show in my style of entertaining. Floral and vegetable motifs always figure prominently in my table settings—not merely in a centerpiece but also in the patterns of the linen and china and stemware and frequently in the details of the room's decor. Not only are botanical motifs lovely to look at, I find they help to establish the mood or theme of a party, whether it's casual, formal, or romantic.

The ideas in this book are intended for all who love botanicals, even if they're not gardeners. Of course, I hope gardeners will find much to inspire them as well. My intent is to encourage new ways of seeing and thinking about flowers, in or out of a vase, in or out of the garden.

Decoration

Cottage in the City

Nearly every urbanite yearns at times for the country—the smell of the earth, the scents and colors of flowers, the open space. Fortunately, a country ambience is as much a state of mind as a state of place. You can take the sensations of the country and transplant them to any plot of land, even a city apartment. In the bedroom of my Manhattan home I wanted to create a retreat, a place where I could tuck in and tune out the world, where I could sit and read, design my fabrics, and paint my watercolors.

While the decorative language of a country house can be translated quite eloquently to a city setting, it may need a little reinterpretation. Most people associate a cottage style with certain clichéd folk elements, such as stenciling

Page 16: *A reproduction Louis XV armchair and a corner chair of scorched bamboo from the late 1800s are placed underneath the windows to form a reading spot. Scorched bamboo was first brought to the Brighton Pavilion, which opened in Brighton, England, in 1826, by the Prince Regent (later to become King George IV) for the first exposition and display of this style of furniture from China and Japan. Corner chairs were made to fit the corner of a room or used as an extra chair in a seating group. (Many antique corner chairs were also commodes— this one is not.)*

Opposite: *The old-fashioned roses in these arrangements include: the 'Belle de Crécy,' a very ruffled lavender rose, which dates back more than three thousand years in Europe; the 'Semi Pera,' or 'White Rose of York,' an alba rose dating back to the Middle Ages and considered to be the hardiest of all old roses; and newer varieties— 'Spectra' (gold-yellow to rust in color), 'Whisky Mac' (bright apricot), 'Jardins de Bagatelle' (creamy white with a hint of pink), 'Brandy' (burnt orange), Iceberg (white), and 'Queen Elizabeth' (pink).*

Following pages: *A blue-and-white color scheme has country overtones. The wallpaper, a periwinkle moiré stripe called Maxima, from my Pretty Rooms collection, establishes the color scheme. Its wavy, silklike watermarks are softer and more elegant than a standard stripe. The room also has a sense of cohesiveness because many of the patterns are floral in some fashion: the print of the curtains, the bedside table skirt, and the botanical decoration on the plates and platters. The sleigh bed, a new piece from my Hill Club collection, is made of rattan—more delicate in style than solid wood.*

and checkered curtains, but a country ambience can also be quite sophisticated. In the eighteenth century, for example, English cottages had both elegance and rough edges: velvet chairs against stucco walls, fine chintzes alongside pine furniture. In the same vein, the cottage-style bedroom in my apartment combines white enamel painted furniture with antiques, and fine pottery with pretty fabrics reminiscent of a country garden.

Flowers are the most immediate and evocative association I have with the country—one of the reasons I design so many botanical patterns and use them so liberally in decorating. That doesn't mean, however, that florals need to be overpowering. Here, in my bedroom, botanical motifs appear subtly in the cutwork lace of the bed linens, in watercolors and engravings, in the print of the curtains, and in the patterned pieces of porcelain that adorn walls, shelves, and tabletops.

It is, in fact, the pottery—the plates, platters, cups—that really establishes the bucolic mood of the room and more specifically its color scheme of blue and white. Blue-and-white captures the essence of fresh air; it is light, and visually calming. In this instance, a blue-and-white striped wallpaper balances the femininity of the florals in the fabrics and provides a backdrop for the pottery hung on the walls. The delicate details of these plates would be lost against a more intricate wallpaper pattern. The pottery, known as transferware because of the process in which the design was applied (see page 97 for a fuller description), often has a botanical design. Up close, you can see that each platter is unique, with a different floral pattern or pastoral scene. From a distance, however, the collection as a whole has an artistic impact.

While there is a lot of visual stimulus in this room, from the porcelain to the curtain fabric to the batik on an armchair, there is also a sense of order emanating from the

blue-and-white color scheme. Though a two-tone color scheme might initially seem limiting, it can actually be a liberating decorating choice. It gives you structure, a framework within which you have license to be creative. Simple white painted furniture is a refreshing change of pace from the sleeker types of furniture typically seen in city bedrooms. Many of the pieces here—such as the hutch, the glass-fronted cupboard, and the little octagonal table—

were originally from old Pennsylvania farmhouses. When I found them, they were not a pleasant sight! The pieces were painted a ghastly shade of orange and covered with decals, yet their simple classic lines were apparent. Stripped and painted with a glossy white lacquer, the furniture was restored to its original charm.

A country style in the city is something of a balancing act. So as not to overdo the whitewashed look, which is somewhat primitive, I also used furniture of rattan and walnut, which adds a note of sophistication. Although some of the pieces are darker than others, none is so heavy that it doesn't work well with the white pieces. There's also a lightness to the design of the rattan bed, the mahogany shelves, and the bamboo Victorian corner chair set beneath the window. The bamboo chair is one of my favorite seats. When I'm having a difficult time designing fabrics in my office, I come home and sit in this chair, clear the nearby table of everything but a pad, paints, and pencils, and begin to sketch some of the flowers that will eventually become fabrics or wallpapers for a new collection.

The generous use of white linens and lace also lends a country air to this city bedroom. Although lace is refined, it is also quintessentially country, perhaps because for centuries lace was made in the countryside. It has a crisp freshness and simplicity, particularly when used against white fabrics or white furniture. There's a subtle delicacy to white-on-white florals—you have to look closely to see the details.

Interest in lace has flourished in recent years, particularly for good-quality antique pieces. Most vintage linens feature beautiful floral motifs and date from the late 1800s (older linens are so fragile that they are mostly found in museums). I am particularly fond of a type of lacy fabric called cutwork, so named because the linen within each hand-embroidered segment was carefully cut out by hand

and the cut edges bound with thread so they wouldn't fray. To linen connoisseurs, modern cutwork from China (most of which is machine-made) lacks the delicacy typical of older work. Still, it is very pretty and certainly more durable than its antique counterparts—an especially important consideration when the linens are adorning a bed.

Most of the bed linens in this room are variations of white—from antique ivory to crisp, new white. Pieces of nineteenth-century lace are draped over tables and used to line shelves in a cupboard. French lace panels grace the windows, as they do so often in European cottages. It's very rare to find antique lace curtains—the combination of laundering and light eventually makes them disintegrate. These modern lace curtains provide a visual screen from the city's glare, yet because they are so diaphanous they allow sunlight to filter through.

Opposite: A country-style hutch with leaded glass doors houses a vast array of blue-and-white children's teacups. White shells, a transferware creamer, and a small Wedgwood pitcher continue the blue-and-white theme.

Lace graces a comfortable club chair, above (in the same moiré stripe as the wallpaper). The larger pillow is cutwork from China. The doily, softening the back of the chair, is from my husband's family.

Following pages: My favorite country roses are the "old-fashioned" variety. These roses—very full and round and dense— were a favorite of nineteenth-century English and French gardeners, and are just now enjoying a resurgence of popularity.

29

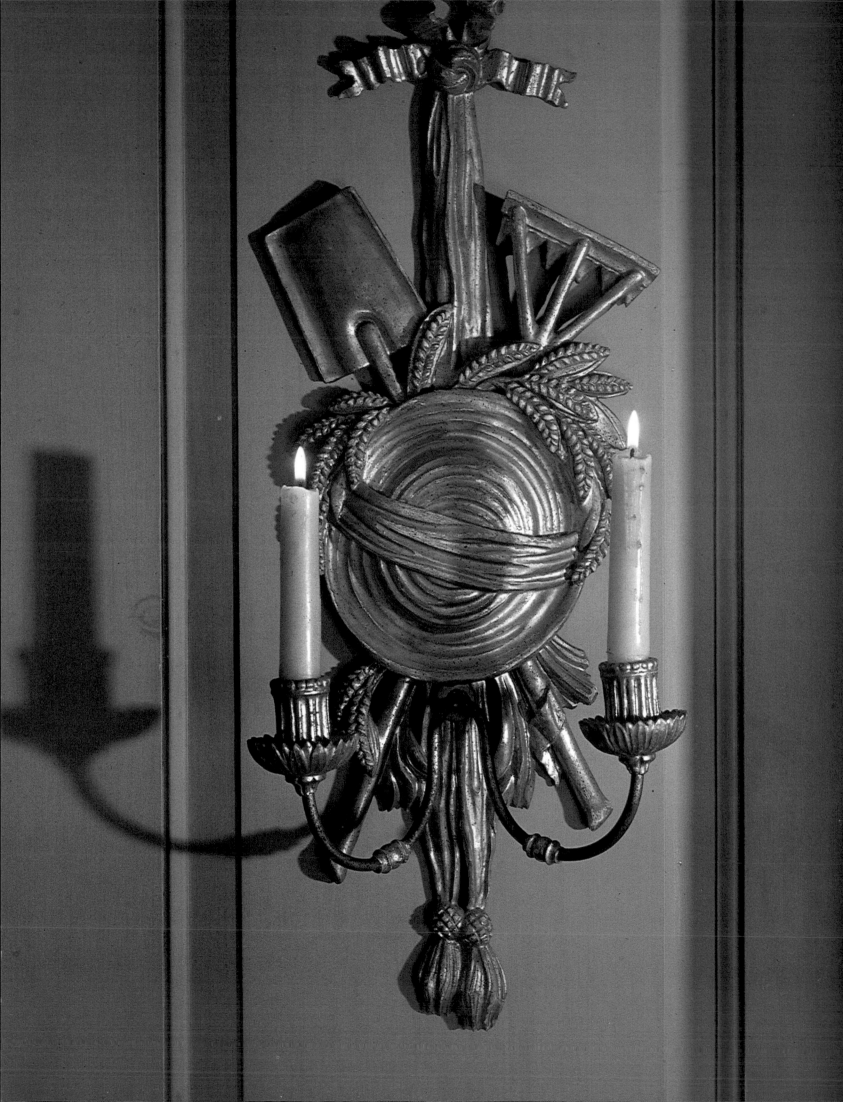

Formal Florals

One of the most graceful homes I've ever visited is that of a leading horticulturalist, my good friend and gardening mentor, Marion Hosmer. In her house on the southern coast of Maine, she has combined her love of beautiful furnishings with her great passion for gardening in such a way that the home is both grand and welcoming. She and her husband, Calvin, built the stone house in the classical style of Queen Anne forty-five years ago, though it looks as though it has been there forever. The Hosmers designed the house according to the direction of the sun's rays, so that there would always be as much light as possible in every room.

The house is a gardener's dream. From the moment you open the front door, you are embraced by the sight and smell of flowers. There is always a magnificent seasonal arrangement on the antique table in the entrance hall. Although the house is filled with interesting pieces of furniture, the flowers and branches gathered from the surrounding gardens and orchards are equally prominent. On almost any given day in the summer Marion Hosmer, who is continually redefining the art of gardening for pleasure, can be found in one of her gardens, dressed in blue jeans and sneakers, with gloves and a spade.

The music room, where Marion plays the piano, is the epitome of understated elegance. When I first saw this room, I was transported. I felt I was in another era. And in fact the room, Marion tells me, has changed very little since they built the house. But what's so remarkable is that it doesn't feel old-fashioned or museumlike. Although most of the furniture is of impeccable Georgian pedigree, each piece also has a story behind it, often a personal one, a family history. Unexpected pieces add warmth and personality, such as an ornately carved stool, eccentric in the best sense of the word, acquired in India in the mid-1800s by Calvin Hosmer's seafaring great-grandfather. The room is also resplendent with personal references to their passion for gardening, such as the gilded sconces adorned with a gardener's hat and rake that flank the fireplace. These are the sorts of details that one notices because the room has been decorated with restraint.

The principle of understatement is also conveyed in the muted palette of the room. The predominant shade is celadon green (a natural shade for a gardener to choose!), which appears in the sofa, the wainscoting, and the curtains. It is also reflected throughout the room by the silvery wallpaper, slightly tarnished by age. The subdued hues lend a hush to the room.

It may seem surprising for an avid gardener to be fond of formal flower arrangements that don't include a single

flower. But Marion, who has won countless garden-club blue ribbons for both conventional and unconventional arrangements, is a proponent of botanicals of all types. In assembling the arrangements that I did here, I followed her example and used only leaves, berries, and flowering branches. Many of the compositions also contain artemisia, a silvery-green foliage that echoes the muted colors of the room. While these botanical elements are not in and of themselves formal, the arrangements—in symmetric groups of two and three vases—have a stately presence.

When it came time to refurbish the guest room in my city apartment, the first image that came to mind was the Hosmers' music room. I wanted to capture that same grace and richness on a more intimate scale.

I find that once you have a mental picture of a certain style (an idea can just as easily come from a painting), it's a matter of adapting it to your taste, your space, and your possessions. For me, that meant creating the bedroom's decor around a trio of export plates—among my favorite porcelains. ("Export" refers to virtually any china that was manufactured during the eighteenth or nineteenth century in China for a foreign market—in this case, England.) The celadon background of these plates suggested the room's wall color; their bouquets and borders inspired the fabric I designed for the curtains and bed linens.

The real focus of the room is, as one would expect, the bed—in this instance, a regal Louis XV design with floral carvings. Perhaps the most opulent element here is the bed's rich gold needlework coverlet, which dates from the 1800s. In its previous life, the cloth was a curtain that had been stored away for decades in my mother's linen closet. If you judge something by its aesthetic potential rather than its perceived purpose, you expand the possibilities of truly creative decorating.

Exotica

Exotic style revels in color, it indulges in ornamentation, and it celebrates the unusual—a piece of furniture with fretwork, a tapestry brought back from another part of the world. While the word "exotic" typically conjures up India and all points east—China, Japan, Thailand—it can be broadened to include any foreign port. An exotic style evokes another place or time; it's expressive and elaborate, and to me it's also quite romantic. Intrinsic to an exotic interior is warmth—a richness of pattern, an exuberance of color. Provenance is not necessarily as important as tone. Eclecticism is in and of itself exotic.

In the living room of my Manhattan apartment I've combined Oriental and Occidental elements. The furniture

Page 46: *A nineteenth-century Chinese whatnot, made of bamboo, is used as a bookshelf. On it hangs a silver sculpture of Mediterranean fruit—a symbol of luck and welcome. On the wall is a paisley shawl, a nineteenth-century interpretation of those from Kashmir.*

An array of silver boxes and tokens displayed on a mahogany nesting table, right: *an Edwardian baby rattle with a coral handle and embossed silver bells with floral motifs; a Chinese carved coral branch and silver hairpin with two jade leaves; an English heart-shaped box from the late 1800s, a gift from my Aunt Mary. The smaller boxes are all silver, most with floral motifs, collected from Mexico to India.*

These begonia-leaf plates, opposite, *which cover an entire wall in the living room of my New York City apartment, are arranged symmetrically around a pastel drawing of the Barber of Seville. The collection grew slowly, each side a mirror image of the other. I would hang a plate only once I'd found a similar piece, which gave me great incentive to search. Many of the plates are not only two of a kind but were by the same painter, identified on the back with a number.*

Exotic twists and turns: a mix of patterns, periods, and details in my Manhattan living room, following pages. *An English sofa with scrolled arms; a Queen Anne chair (upholstered in yellow jacquard) with swan-neck arms; a pair of Dutch armchairs with spiraled arms and legs. The parrot-tulip balloon shades with their scalloped edges have an undulating wave effect; the pinked ruffle mimics the sheared edges of the parrot tulips on the coffee table. The fringe on the footstool echoes the tassels that provide the pattern for the table skirts. A gilded American mirror from the 1800s, carved with floral rosettes, is flanked by my botanical watercolors of daffodils and day lilies framed in silver leaf.*

is of disparate origins and periods—Chinese, Japanese, European, and American—some antique, others reproduction. The room is also full of a mélange of objects I've collected on my travels, as well as the fabrics these objects have inspired me to design. And there's almost always the scent of sandalwood incense in the air. Exotic as the ambience is, however, the room feels like home because it is filled with things that I feel comfortable with and adore.

To give the room the feeling of warmth, I chose a soft pink wall color, which I find warmer than white. Many people shy away from pink because they assume it will look overly sweet and feminine, but it needn't. The effect of pink walls depends on the other decorative elements in the room. Here the pink is offset by vivid hues in the furnishings. All the chairs, for instance, are covered in jewel tones: deep pink and gold damask or red velvet or old floral tapestry needlepoint. I collect chairs and footstools for precisely this reason—because they are great showcases for colorful and interesting fabrics.

The advantage of pink in a pale shade is that, like white or beige, it acts as a neutral; against such an unobtrusive background, colorful collections and objects are thrown into

relief. The majolica hung on the walls becomes, in effect, the room's wallpaper. It's a matter of juxtaposition. The same principle works in reverse: If I were to paint the walls an intense color, like Chinese Red, I would choose pale or neutral tones for the decorative elements.

Patterns of different scales and sensibilities mix easily in an exotic interior. If you were to actually count, you'd find more than twenty different textile patterns in this living room. Windows, in particular, offer an opportunity to present an expanse of pattern and color. In this room, where the windows cover two entire walls, the curtains in a bold parrot-tulip print are the dominant influence. If you're going to choose a pattern this strong, however, you have to be sure you really love it. For me, these large florals are a pleasure to look at; they remind me of the spectacular tulip gardens in Amsterdam.

52

Patterns intermingle in less obvious ways, too, in this room. Every one of the rugs, for instance, has a different design, and the wooden parquet floor that is visible between the carpets creates a pattern of its own. Along with the mix of pattern, there is a variety of textures—velvet, needlepoint, silk, damask—adding tactile interest.

With so many disparate design elements, it helps to have some threads of continuity, subtle though they may be. The turquoise, green, and pink colors of the majolica plates, for instance, are deliberately repeated in the upholstered furniture. On either side of the sofa are matching lamps with bases shaped like monkeys; each monkey holds a type of porcelain fruit known as peach abundance—the same type of decorative fruit sculpture that adorns the lowboy and butler's tray table.

A profusion of pattern tends to make a room appear

A Chinese black lacquered rosewood chair
embellished with sunflower motifs,
which dates from Victorian times, is one of
the most comfortable seats in
the room, opposite.

My favorite footstool is the lacquered
Chinese opium ottoman with a secret
drawer in one of its panels and a cushion
made from a paisley shawl from France.

An ode to the Orient, following pages: red
lacquer tea boxes, pieces of wood
carvings with floral motifs, exotic carved
beads in the shape of flowers, and
Tibetan prayer beads with the two larger
beads in the shape of flowers.

smaller, which isn't necessarily a drawback if you like the coziness of a close space. As a rule, the higher the ceiling, the more strength of pattern the room can carry. (The ceilings in my living room are over ten feet high.) No matter what the dimensions of a room are, when virtually every surface and every wall space is richly decorated, the interior takes on an exotic identity. It becomes a world unto itself.

Summer House Charm

A summer house, either in reality or in memory, engages all the senses: We smell the freshly mown grass or the salty brine of the ocean; we see the lush colors of the garden; we feel the warmer breezes blowing in. . . .

There is a natural flow between inside and outside. Windows are typically open and doors left ajar. A summer house is in fact open in every way. The interiors tend to be airy and uncluttered. Light, pale colors predominate and foster an expansive, cool atmosphere. Floral patterns also suit a summer house; botanical motifs, after all, are inspired by a country landscape. What's more—floral fabrics and papers look wonderful when they've been softened and faded by the sun of long summer days.

Page 58: This gazebo is more properly termed a belvedere, because it is attached to the house rather than freestanding—an example of shingle-style whimsy. From inside there's a view of spectacular sunsets up the river.

The Donnellys' majestic shingle-style house, named Lane's End, right, *was built in 1890 on the banks of the York River and has been in their family for three generations. The view from nearly every window is of the picturesque harbor.*

A basket of potted pansies on the table in the front hall welcomes guests to the Donnelly home, opposite. *The large diamond-paned windows are original to the house and typical of shingle-style architecture. They throw sunny patterns into the hall all afternoon. The umbrella stand is really an old leather fire bucket, which years ago would be filled with water from the river and passed up to the house, brigade-style, until help arrived.*

A lived-in living room with a past, following pages: *The desk was made from three-hundred-year-old maple by the owner's grandfather. The Victorian settee in the corner and the pale-blue antique sofa have been a part of the house for as long as anyone can remember. Much of the library holds inherited books; some volumes date back to the early 1800s. The room is also filled with the most personal items of history—old photo albums and family pictures.*

One of the most enchanting settings for a summer house is York Harbor, Maine. My friend Carol Donnelly has a shingle-style home that overlooks the harbor itself, and from almost every window you can see sweeps of sky or water.

The overriding feeling of the interior is one of relaxed elegance, for a summer house, however grand, is at its heart informal. It is designed around the principle of livability, the notion of ease. The Donnellys fully expect that their friends and neighbors (not to mention their dogs) are going to track in some of the outdoors—the sand, the leaves—with them. They have adopted a rational approach to decorating that accommodates their summer life with style.

While the Donnellys have kept the living room relatively simple, they have not stinted on comfort. There's a soft rug underfoot, there are many places to sit, and cushions in every chair. Nothing is too ordered, too finished, too perfect—a piece of old fabric is draped over the sofa, books are piled on the tables. There's a kind of visual ease as well: soft blues, greens, and pinks mix easily with whites and neutrals. These are the soothing colors of summer.

Whenever the weather is fine, the Donnellys are on the

porch—mornings, afternoons, evenings. The wide white porch is bordered by peonies and white rosa rugosa shrubs, whose fragrance is in the air all summer long. The porch, which turns into a belvedere at one end, is in effect a room poised half inside and half outside, a bridge to both worlds. This hybrid space has the attributes of an interior, pared down to the essentials. What's there is simple and informal—painted white benches, Adirondack chairs, and wicker chairs, all of which hold up to the elements. But style is not abandoned. A round wicker table is dressed with an embroidered tea cloth. Vintage chintz pillows add color and pattern, as do the colorful pitchers filled with fresh flowers. The real decoration, of course, is the stunning harbor view.

In the Donnelly dining room, opposite, *an old iron urn holds rhododendron. A late-1800s transferware platter in an unusual teal blue has been embellished with hand-painted flowers. The small ginger jar was discovered in the house when it was purchased three generations ago—part of its "dowry." The floral embroidered tea cloth dates from the turn of the century.*

Old Adirondack chairs, above, *entice one to sit and look out over the harbor at the fishing boats, lobster boats, and sailboats passing by.*

The broad rambling porch, following pages, *is comfortably furnished. Peonies and rosa rugosa are planted below, and their fragrance wafts up to the porch.*

Previous pages: *Pillows have long had a place on porches—they add a bit of softness to the garden furniture, and a bit of pattern to a traditionally all-white color scheme. If the pillows are made of vintage chintz, so much the better. The floral fabric is a visual reminder of lush country gardens.*

Crossways, the shingle-style house down the road from the Donnellys', right, *has always been painted Yankee red.*

A *sweet botanical touch,* opposite: *An old country chair is embellished with hand-painted florals.*

Following pages: *The Crossways dining room—informal and inviting. All the woodwork is painted pale gray, the shade of weathered driftwood. With a simple rug on the floor and an unobtrusive geometric paper on the walls, the botanical flourishes stand out.*

Pages 74–75: *The two guest bedrooms at Crossways are similar in structure and furnishings—but there's one difference: the wall covering. One is painted pale blue; the other has floral wallpaper that has faded over time. The two rooms are undeniably distinct in feeling.*

Pages 76–77: *another charming bedroom, uncluttered yet warm. A pretty floral wallpaper, over fifty years old, is a focal point of the room and provides a lush backdrop for a white chenille bedspread. Against the white furniture, the flowers are particularly striking.*

Grandeur, however, is not a prerequisite for great style. In a lovely shingle-style cottage called Crossways, also in York Harbor, summer-house charm is epitomized by a pair of simple and functional guest bedrooms. The rooms are sparsely furnished, with no extraneous detail, no distractions. The effect is unstudied and refreshing.

One bedroom is a study in white—furniture, bedspread, rug, chair, curtains. Even the vase on the bureau is creamy white and filled with white flowers. The walls are light: a pale, pale blue, which gives the sensation of sky. There's a serenity to the room, and a cozy feel, in part because of the sloped ceiling and dormers. There's also a warmth from the pine floors and the casual country furniture.

Another guest bedroom, right next door, has the same genteel, unpretentious style—a maple bed, white painted bureau, and chenille bedspread. The real difference is in the floral wall covering, which adds a romantic quality to the room. While the pattern is colorful, the colors themselves are subdued—muted tones of rose pink and gray blue on a background the color of old linen. Because the print is an overall pattern, it's easy on the eyes. When you lie back on the bed, you feel totally enveloped by flowers.

70

Private Corners

Most of us, without even realizing it, seek out one particular spot when we want to be alone—to read or write a letter, to relax, to daydream, a private corner where we feel most comfortable, both physically and psychologically. That corner isn't always private in the strict sense of the word, but it has a *feeling* of privacy, a sense of solitude or serenity. It's a place to feel territorial about, a place to indulge whims and express a personal sense of aesthetics.

For one person, the ideal spot is austere and simple, stripped of fussy details; for another, clutter may bring the most comfort. For some, a retreat must be dark and quiet; for others, the prerequisite is natural light and a view—a window seat, perhaps, that looks out over a cityscape.

Page 78: An old, weathered Adirondack chair and table in front of my perennial garden in Maine is a serene spot to enjoy a cup of tea at day's end.

A window seat, right, *is a time-honored daydreamer's spot. This one, in a cottage in York Harbor, Maine, is perched on the landing halfway up the stairs. It's a perfect place to pause, have a cup of tea and read a book, write a note, or simply gaze out the window. The window seat is covered in a vintage chintz, and the teacup has a floral design. The grandfather "clock" is actually a Victorian hat and umbrella stand that was upended and painted as a whimsical trompe l'oeil timepiece.*

My friend Lynn Eaton has devoted a room in her house in Maine to the study of horticulture. The bench and bookcase, opposite, *are both piled high with books on gardening. For Lynn, this is a place to gather ideas and plan her gardens.*

A grand chair in the corner is rich with botanical decoration, following pages: *Antiques dealer Lynn Chase has created an intimate reading spot surrounded by bookcases. Floor-to-ceiling windows provide natural light by day; a pharmacy lamp provides illumination at night. The nearby desk is covered with gardening anthologies.*

Pages 84–85: A great expanse of lawn can also seem very private. Here, a pretty parasol shelters a simple teatime repast and lends a touch of formality and elegance to the setting.

The best private corners make us feel soothed, pampered in some way. I have a friend who considers the bathtub her true sanctuary. The water's heat, the scent of the bath oil, the sensation of being immersed (literally and figuratively)—all combine to make her feel as though she has created a private little world that only she inhabits.

The point about a private corner is to please oneself. In my personal retreats I am surrounded by things that have meaning. One such "corner" is a small table in the green-and-white sitting room of my Manhattan apartment. This is where I like to paint my watercolors; the color scheme of the room reminds me of a garden. In our country

A peaceful spot under the staircase in my house in Maine, opposite. The sloped ceiling gives the corner a built-in coziness and even more of a sense of enclosure. A very comfortable, oversized chair is wearing a chintz slipcover for summer (the winter version is more formal). There's a good reading lamp close by and plump old pillows covered with an overblown floral fabric. The chair is flanked by a side table and a large basket that also serves as a table. The lamp has a birch-log base and a shade decorated with cutout fabric flowers. A bamboo bookcase holds paints, gardening books, and found treasures.

Left: *a private place at Suzy Verrier's rose farm, Forevergreen Farm, in Maine. Nature has been allowed to grow unimpeded and form a natural awning for a trio of Adirondack chairs.*

Following pages: *A cement bench nestled between arborvitae shrubs at the Hosmers' is an elegant and austere resting spot—not so much the kind of place to linger as a place to pause in the shade.*

house in Maine I have another refuge—an overstuffed chair tucked beneath the staircase, where I love to sit and pore over gardening books.

The term "private corner" should be interpreted rather loosely. A corner need not be indoors at all or, for that matter, even have walls. A private retreat can be carved out of air—a wooden bench under a tree, perhaps, where the shade provides a sense of intimacy and nothing intrudes but the sounds of nature. For a gardener, the most pleasant spot might be as simple as a chair pulled up next to the flower bed. Still another kind of refuge might be found in a vast open space—an empty stretch of beach, or a meadow of wildflowers.

Collections

Although floral motifs have graced botanical objects for centuries, the golden age of decorative ornamentation was in late-eighteenth-century Europe. At the forefront of the movement was the French court watercolorist Pierre-Joseph Redouté, whose beautifully rendered, finely detailed paintings of roses and other flowers inspired a profusion of floral motifs.

Once I began collecting objects with a botanical theme, the possibilities seemed endless: brightly colored majolica pottery fashioned after flowers, leaves, or vegetables; Oriental sculptures in the shape of fruit; antique boxes engraved with floral motifs; and china decorated with lyrical, pastoral scenes.

Part of the joy of collecting, aside from the treasures

Two begonia-leaf plates flank a platter with a sunflower motif in its center, page 90. *On the antique drop-leaf table is more of my majolica collection: pitchers of various sizes, butter pats, small nut dishes, and plates. The bright pink of the open sugar bowl's interior is typical of majolica. The candlesticks are actual ostrich eggs.*

Opposite: a festive display of brightly colored majolica. On the top shelf: a platter decorated with artichokes and white asparagus, three pitchers with botanical motifs, and a box decorated with asparagus spears, a very traditional French majolica motif. On the second tier: asparagus plates, each of which is hand-painted and unique. (A sheaf of dried lavender adds an air of the French countryside.) On the bottom shelf: three graduated pitchers, found in off-the-beaten-path antiques stores.

Following pages: a detail of the begonia-leaf majolica plates on the wall of my New York apartment.

themselves, is the search. In a way, collections acquired while traveling are a record of where you've been. While many people collect purely for investment (to have the best, oldest, most authentic), I look for a different kind of value. To me, a collection is very personal—it's a reflection of taste. One piece of ceramic fruit is incidental; five is an aesthetic statement.

It's easy to fall in love with the type of pottery called majolica. And no wonder—majolica is bright and enchantingly childlike, and it has a colorful history. A Victorian revival of the Italian Renaissance ceramic called *maiolica*, majolica is earthenware that's been modeled in bold relief and coated with vibrant low-fire glazes. The naive quality of majolica is not surprising once you know that many of the pieces, particularly those made in America, were painted by young girls working in the pottery factories.

At the time it was introduced, some traditionalists found majolica crude, unsophisticated, even vulgar, because of its garish hues (turquoises, pinks, reds, and greens) and also because it was so commonplace. During the 1880s in the United States, majolica plates were given away at the A&P grocery store with a purchase of baking soda. But now, more than a century later, majolica has a fresh appeal. I like to think of majolica as the Fauvist art of ceramics. And in fact I treat the pottery like art; I've devoted almost an entire wall in my apartment to my collection of plates, which are in the shape of begonia leaves.

The majority of majolica is botanical in nature. Along with begonia-leaf plates, you can find platters adorned with sunflowers, pitchers shaped like tree trunks, and plates embossed with white asparagus—a vegetable grown primarily in Europe. Some of the most whimsical majolica pieces are decorated according to their purpose—fruit motifs on fruit plates, corncob shapes on a corn-syrup pitcher.

As available as majolica once was, now you really have

to search for it. To me that's a challenge: part of the pleasure of collecting, after all, is foraging through heaps of objects at a flea market to find one wonderful piece lurking in the pile. Fortunately, majolica's bold colors are easy to spot, though it is difficult to find pieces in mint condition. The glazes that were used to make majolica were brittle, and after years of use they tended to chip or crack. However, I appreciate the little nick or the discoloration—it's part of an object's past and proof that the piece was really used at one time.

Where the vivid hues of majolica are cheerful, the universally appealing color combination of blue and white has an understated charm. As far back as 1740, the British East India Trading Company sought blue-and-white pottery from ports all over the world to satisfy the huge demand for it at home. Eventually, the British applied these colors to a type of pottery known as transferware, a reference to the decorative process: A design was engraved on a copper plate, printed on strong paper with a warm, oily ink, and then pressed—that is, transferred—onto the pottery before the ink dried. Then the paper was removed and the pottery was fired in a kiln. Because the transfers were applied by hand, the pattern would often be a bit off-center. To me, this imperfection only makes the pieces more interesting.

Of all the many varieties of blue-and-white patterns created both in Europe and Asia, I'm most attracted to English printed pottery, because of its botanical decoration. The English have always been mad about gardens, and from the mid-eighteenth century to the present they've used plates and platters as a canvas for floral motifs or pastoral scenes. These scenes often reflected current events: During the long occupation by England of India and parts of Africa, for example, palm trees, elephants, and zebras began to appear on the pottery.

A plethora of majolica on display in the sitting room of my apartment, opposite: plates, pitchers, saucers, and bowls, ranging in decorative motifs from leaves to flowers to pineapples to sheaves of wheat. Most of these pieces were found along the Eastern seaboard at antiques shows and flea markets, and many bear the stamp of the Griffin, Smith and Hill factory in Phoenixville, Pennsylvania, where some of the most colorful American majolica was made. The factory doors were open from 1879 to 1902, but it was really in the 1880s that the majolica craze peaked. The pottery here is arranged with an eye to height, the tallest pieces in the back.

Because the color scheme is easy on the eyes, blue-and-white transferware is ideal for display. Still, I periodically shift and rearrange the pieces so that I can look at them from different angles and new perspectives. Like a garden, a collection periodically needs tending, weeding out. Plates that were on the wall in the bedroom may get retired to a cupboard; teacups that were stored in a glass hutch might take a more visible place on a side table or lowboy.

Old or antique pieces of blue-and-white transferware have more than an aesthetic value, however; platters, plates, and cups can also be pressed into practical service. One Thanksgiving was saved from near disaster because of my pottery collection. The turkey was ready to be carved when I realized that I had no platter for it (all my platters were in our country house in Maine). My husband reminded me of the blue-and-white platter on the library wall. Of course! Down it came and served us admirably. It's natural to regard objects that are very old as very fragile. But if you think about it, the piece has already lasted a hundred years, so there's no reason to expect it won't last another century.

While blue-and-white was the original and most pervasive of the transferware color schemes, other colors were soon introduced. In Victorian times there was a surge of new eye-catching combinations: red and green, green and blue, green and purple, and brown and green. Multicolored transferware is harder to find—there simply wasn't that much of it made—and it is five times as expensive as blue-and-white. Because the color combinations aren't seen that often, they strike the eye as novel.

The transferware technique was also applied to tiles, which were used throughout the Victorian years and well into the Edwardian period in England. They were made in a variety of styles, colors, motifs, and designs—with the

A cupboard is full of decorative bowls that
have a functional role in the tea service,
opposite and following pages.
Called waste bowls, they were used from
Victorian times onward as receptacles for
loose or cool tea after the brewing
process. They come in a variety of sizes and
motifs (from wild roses to pastoral
scenes to roosters in a barnyard). My collection is ninety percent English—not
surprising considering that the English, with
their love of tea, produced a great
number of tea sets.

emphasis on botanicals—and were used for fireplace surrounds and as backsplashes for washstands. Until quite recently, these tiles were fairly accessible at minimal cost in England; lately they have been more difficult to find, particularly the more elaborately designed ones.

One of the most beautiful types of china I collect is from the Far East. It's called Chinese export, an umbrella term for any sort of porcelain made and painted in China in the eighteenth and nineteenth centuries, then shipped to other countries (including Spain, Holland, England, France, Scandinavia, and, much later, the United States). Since export was disseminated all over the world, pieces of it can be found in many different places today. The export china I've collected tends to be very delicate in color (pinks and lilacs on a celadon ground) and in design —each piece was hand-painted, many with little birds and butterflies, or, my favorite, romantically rendered flowers and garlands.

Some botanical treasures from the East are purely decorative. Porcelain sculptures in the shape of fruits have been made since the Ming dynasty and are prevalent in Buddhist countries. These handmade pieces include peaches, pumpkins, pomegranates, and even one called Buddha's hand (a fruit not eaten but picked for its fragrance). The older porcelains are extraordinarily rare and expensive, though sculptures from the late nineteenth and early twentieth centuries are still available and relatively affordable, and have the same sensual appeal. There are also current reproductions that are true to the old style, though I prefer the patina that comes with age. (A little bit of white vinegar rubbed on the fruit will separate the truly antique from the merely made-to-look-old pieces.)

To me, a most elegant style of ceramic is creamware —a buff-colored pottery with a transparent glaze. Creamware objects range from plates and platters to ornate cache-

A *detail of a collection of Chinese stoneware fruits on a Queen Anne lowboy,* right.

This collection of creamware, opposite, *dating from the eighteenth century, was acquired over many years. A dinner service lines the back of the cupboard. The rest of the collection consists of small eclectic pieces, many of which are unglazed, a type of creamware that is more and more difficult to find.*

pots and floral sculptures. The decorative detail is added not with color but with elaborate raised embellishment, often of a botanical nature. The earthenware, perfected by Josiah Wedgwood, was created in 1762 and was also known as Queensware, in honor of Queen Charlotte, who was particularly fond of it.

In a different medium altogether is English-created mercury glass, also known as "silvered" glass, or "poor man's silver." The glass, which is often painted with botanical detail, emits a lovely ethereal glow and has a luster that is warmer than silver. Mercury glass was first made in England in the mid-1800s, and shortly thereafter in the United States. Today, collectors prize it and it takes some searching to find pieces that are intact. Although mercury glass is no longer made in the same way, some modern manufacturers, particularly in Mexico, are approximating

the process in a cruder fashion with unintended bubbles in the glass. To my eye, there's no replacement for the original.

Ultimately, no matter how prized or rare a collection, its value goes unappreciated if it is not displayed—and displayed to advantage. Plates and platters, for instance, look striking hung on a wall, a relatively simple process. Plate hangers that hook inconspicuously around the rim of a plate are sold in hardware stores, in a variety of sizes to fit a very small dessert plate or an oversized platter.

Virtually any surface—a tabletop, bookcase, shelf, or windowsill—can be turned into a still life. I find that the best way to approach the composition is to organize the objects by color or shape or by cultural origin. There are pragmatic considerations as well when it comes to display-ing objects on a surface, such as a coffee table—leaving enough room for a cup of tea to be set down, for instance. It makes sense to avoid placing objects on a table that's right next to a chair, where someone could easily sit down and knock them over with an elbow. The point is, although you want a collection to be seen, you don't want it to interfere with anyone's comfort.

If, however, I intend a table to be used for the sole purpose of showing a collection, I deliberately place the table out of the way of traffic. And when it comes to objects that are truly precious (even if only to me), they are placed out of reach, on high shelves or the tops of cabinets, or placed behind the glass doors of a vitrine.

With certain valuable objects there's no need to be so protective. Silver, for instance, is virtually accident-proof; while it's possible to put a ding in it if it is dropped, it's almost impossible to break. The large ceramic fruit sculp-tures that I collect are also quite sturdy. I keep them out on the coffee table, where they can be both touched and admired.

An array of mercury glass, opposite: This type of silvered glass has less shine than silver, more sheen than pewter. An assortment of vases, compotes, goblets, and pitchers dates from the late nineteenth century; they were acquired in antiques shops in Maine.

The delicacy of Chinese export is perfectly suited to a tea service, following pages. This set made for the English market consists of slightly varying floral patterns and a mix of bowls and cups of different sizes. All the pieces share the same color scheme, however— pinks and greens and lilacs against a celadon background, typical of export ware. The grand vases are also export and date from the early 1800s. They are always filled—sometimes with flowers, sometimes with leaves. In this case the vases hold eucalyptus leaves, which have an invigorating scent.

Gardens

The Flower Garden

A flower garden is, in a sense, a form of design, a reflection of one's artistic sense. Colors, textures, and shapes play much the same role in a garden as they do on a canvas. The connection between these two creative arts—painting and gardening—has a long history. Monet's gardens at Giverny, in Normandy, were an extension of his studio; he carefully planted with an eye to color and composition. Renoir lived amid a pastoral paradise at his farm near the Mediterranean with both formal rose gardens and meadows of bright wildflowers. Painter-turned-gardener Gertrude Jekyll was a dominant force in horticulture throughout the early 1900s. Her ideas about color balance—the importance of juxtaposing bright hues with gentler ones, for instance—became the basis for

An inviting entrance to the garden, page 116: *a bright mélange of cone flowers with daisylike blooms.*

Right: *gardening implements, a mix of old and new—a claw, a few spades, a spike called a dibble for planting bulbs, another circular bulb planter, and several pairs of shears.*

The aesthetics of gardening extend to the tools, opposite. *The simple strong lines of utilitarian rakes, hoes, and shovels create a striking image against a shed door.*

Following pages: *an unstructured perennial garden. By following the form of the land, the flower beds create the outline of the garden. The stone wall, hand-assembled from fieldstone found on the property, looks as if it has always been there.*

A subtle blue-and-white color scheme in this section of the garden creates a tranquil look, *pages 122–123. The blooms include lilies, balloon flowers, pansies, and astilbe.*

the naturalistic English country garden style, which is still very popular with gardeners on both sides of the Atlantic.

As in any art, the qualities that make for beauty in a garden are highly subjective. You bring to a garden your own sensibilities, feelings, memories. You know best how large a garden you want to maintain, what colors give you pleasure, and in terms of design, whether you like symmetry or asymmetry, order or a little bit of chaos.

The first aesthetic consideration in designing a garden is shape. How you approach that choice is not unlike deciding on the shape of a pool; it depends on how you instinctively feel about a particular form. Some people are drawn to the elegance of ovals; others prefer the structure and order of rectangles; and still others like free-form design.

Often the style of the house serves as inspiration for the shape and sensibility of the garden. An old Colonial, for example, might suggest a picket-fenced perennial border and a rose-covered arbor. A house in the Queen Anne style seems to beg for a formal garden, complete with stone walls, topiary, and sculpted boxwood. But any rules of garden design can be successfully flouted; for example, a

classic oval-shaped English garden forms a surprisingly delightful counterpoint to an angular contemporary house.

Once the basic garden shape is determined, it is filled in with color, which gives the garden its true character. While the prospect of choosing colors among the hundreds of varieties of flowers might seem daunting, it's less so if you think in terms of the four broad color categories into which all flowers fall: blue (lavenders, purples, mauves); pink (salmons, roses, reds); yellow (oranges, lemons, and golds); and white.

The tone and mood of a garden can be modulated through the choice of colors—or of a single color. An all-white garden, for instance, with phlox, lilium, balloon flowers, achillea, and marguerites, is quite formal and looks especially heavenly in the moonlight. An amalgamation of bright hues, as in my own flower garden, creates a mood of exuberance.

The third element of any flower garden design is height, or rather the varying heights of all the blooms. Since taller plants can easily overshadow smaller ones, it makes sense to place the tallest ones at the rear of the garden, where they can form a picturesque backdrop, and plant smaller varieties toward the front. If the garden happens to be oval or circular in shape, then taller plants can be positioned in the middle.

There's yet another criterion for choosing flowers, and that is timing. In the ideal garden something is always in bloom; one flower is bursting forth just as another is beginning to fade. This takes some forethought. In my flower garden, I have devised a timetable in which perennials bloom from the first day of spring well through September. The first flowers out are columbine, with their little yellow hats, and the very early Dutch iris in light shell pink and deep purple. By midsummer, the majority of the garden is in full bloom: there's a profusion of lavender, foxglove,

Opposite above: *A single red poppy stands out next to blue and white lupine.*

The strength of a large bed of a single color, opposite below: *A rudbeckia, when allowed to grow almost untamed, has the impact of an expanse of wildflowers.*

Following pages: *Stepping into the garden one sees sculptured boxwood shrubs and riotous beds of iris and day lilies.*

A collection of vividly colored day lilies in many different hues, pages 128–129. *The lilies have been timed so one variety is always in bloom, from early summer to early fall.*

coreopsis, santolina, and day lily, with its bursts of peach and yellow. As summer ends and fall begins, the garden is still very much alive with color. Chrysanthemums in unusual, sophisticated hues are still blooming into September, and so is one of my favorite perennials, sedum, with its large, splayed leaves and pretty florets with red, pink, and white blossoms.

Not everyone has time to keep up an elaborate flower garden on a daily basis. Many of us have only weekends

free, or sporadic stretches of time during a summer. But that doesn't preclude the pleasures of flower gardening, as long as you keep your plot of land small and manageable and open up the definition of a garden. There's no reason a garden must be in the backyard, for instance. Flowers can line a walkway or flank the front door, where they make a decorative impact and greet you each time you arrive home.

Bulbs are a boon to weekend gardeners, because they require next to no maintenance. They are placed in the ground in the fall, and the colorful flowers burst forth in spring. The season ends, the bulbs survive another winter, and come spring, the process begins again. Many bulbs continue to bloom for up to five years with little tending. My favorite bulbs are jonquils, daffodils, and crocuses. Tulips, on the other hand, while lovely to look at, are tempting

Santolina, lavender, a red astilbe, and a white astilbe in the background, opposite.

'Nadezhda' lilac are pale in color and incredibly fragrant, above.

food for deer and mice. I try to salvage as many blooms as I can each spring before they're eaten.

Many annual plants also do well on a weekend schedule, and have the advantage of being inexpensive and easy to grow. And though they last only one season, it's a long season, from late spring to early fall. Annuals can be grown from seed (rewarding but time-consuming) or bought as small plants from a nursery, which is what I generally do. Like many northern states, Maine has a short growing season, so buying young plants and placing them directly into the ground gives the flowers a head start.

Of the multitudes of annuals, I find I keep coming back to certain flowers, time and again:

Cosmos has large, daisylike flowers in a burst of glowing color. It also has the advantage of being quick-growing. Cosmos will reach over five feet tall, making the flowers an ideal backdrop in a garden.

Nicotiana is delicate-looking, of medium height, and has fragrant trumpet-shaped blossoms. It is available in a range of hues from white to crimson.

Marigold, one of the most resilient of annuals, grows from half a foot tall to three feet. It has a built-in defense against dry weather—the crinkly, buttonlike flowers open slowly, so they are able to hold a store of water inside.

Impatiens, too, are nearly fail-safe. Despite the name, these low bushy plants with bright flowers take little patience, require little attention, and last until the first frost. Impatiens are so adaptable, in fact, that they thrive in the shade and need to be watered only during dry spells.

Morning glories—bright, open-faced, and fast-growing —are one of my favorites. They're natural climbers, perfect for adorning a fence or framing a doorway. Morning glories may shoot up four to six inches in a single day—and up to fifteen feet during a single summer, a sight that delights me every year.

Culinary herbs, opposite from the top: *summer savory, variegated pineapple mint, scented lemon geranium.*

Page 172: *more herbs cultivated for their culinary properties—dill, green sage in flower, tarragon.* Page 173: *more culinary herbs.* Clockwise from the top: *rosemary, sweet marjoram, English thyme, and coriander with coriander seeds.*

- *Basil* is one of my favorites. It is prized for its sweet, clovelike scent and its large, bright-green, oval leaves. I also plant a variety named 'Purple Opal' basil, which has crinkly leaves.

- *Thyme*, another favorite, comes in many varieties, including lemon, orange, and silver. I'm particularly fond of English thyme and grow it next to an old tree stump in my vegetable garden, where it creates a woodland effect.

- *Chives*, with their tall, graceful stalks that bend with the breeze, are another lovely addition to the garden. Chives do, however, have an aggressive growing habit, and without periodical dividing they can overpower a small garden.

- *Parsley*, on the other hand, is easy to contain. Its rich green curly-edged leaves grow in neat, compact rows, making it a natural border for a vegetable garden or pathway.

- *Rosemary*, too, lends itself to a manicured look; for centuries it has been shaped into formal topiaries. The herb's needlelike leaves and purplish flowers stand out against the other plantings in a vegetable garden.

- *Dill* also provides visual contrast when interspersed with vegetables in a garden. Its feathery green plumage, which has delicate flowering heads, can grow up to four feet tall, giving the herb a definitive presence.

- *Sweet marjoram*, pretty to look at, is also known for its intoxicating fragrance. In ancient Rome, the velvety gray-green leaves were scattered on the floor to perfume the air. These days, sweet marjoram is often mixed into potpourri—it's the one ingredient that's difficult to identify.

Certain herbs are prized more for their fragrance than for their flavor. A perfect example is lavender, the oils of which are used in many perfumes and soaps. While lav-

*Creeping thyme doing what it does best—
creeping between the stones on the
garden path, opposite.*

Left: *Variegated pineapple mint, with its
smooth, bright, yellow-splashed leaves,
makes a dramatic contrast to the
neighboring 'Wichita Blue' juniper.*

ender is perhaps most often associated with the south of
France, where it is grown in great profusion, the shrub is
also adaptable—I find it takes quite well to northern
climates.

Of the many varieties of lavender, I'm partial to one
called 'Hidcote,' which has tall wheatlike stems and deep
purple flowers, and another known as 'Munstead,' a shorter
variety with very pale lavender flowers. I've planted both
varieties in the center of my perennial garden, where they
make a charming focal point. Sometimes, while tending
the garden, I'll stop and crush some of the blossoms between my fingers, which releases the oils and fills the air
with a heavenly aroma.

One of the strongest scents comes from lavender cotton,
also known as santolina. I happen to like the aroma, but
moths apparently don't: I find that a few sprigs hung in
the closet are quite useful in keeping the moths away. The
shape of santolina is similar to that of coral; its sturdy gray
or green foliage is topped by small buttonlike flowers. The
herb was used in Victorian England to create "knot" gardens, in which two shades of santolina were planted and
trimmed in an intricate overlapping pattern. In my own

garden, I use santolina as a pretty edging around the perennial garden, where its pungent odor serves as a natural repellent to pests.

Some herbs are best known—and grown—as ground covers. Sweet woodruff is one of the prettiest in this category: its delicate leaves are shaped like tiny umbrellas, each topped by a white flower. Creeping thyme grows only an inch or two high, and its tiny flowers bloom almost all summer long. I planted it around the inner perimeter of my flower garden, and true to its name, it has begun creeping onto the path inside the garden. I leave it in place rather than trim it back—with each step a heady fragrance is released.

The wonderful thing about herbs is that they have a life beyond their growing season. Many can be dried and preserved. While home-dried herbs are not as flavorful as fresh, they're still far superior to the store-bought variety. Herbs should be harvested before their flowers are fully open, when the essential oils are at their peak. It's also best to gather them on a dry day early in the morning, before the midday sun has sapped them of their flavor.

Of all the ways to preserve herbs, I prefer the simplest: air drying. In this process, you tie whole stems or branches together and hang them upside down indoors until the leaves are crisp and ready to use. Herbs dry quickly—in less than two weeks. Once they are dry, you can store them in airtight glass jars; they'll keep in a cool, dark cupboard for several seasons.

Herbs can also be preserved by using them to flavor oil or vinegar. Some of the best herbs for this process are rosemary, thyme, and marjoram. The process is effortless: A sprig is immersed in the liquid, and then the jar or bottle is tightly covered; after a week or two the flavor of the herb will have infused the oil or vinegar. Placed in attractive containers, these make lovely gifts.

of knowing the exposures and selecting the plants that will do the best under the light conditions you have. The most consistent and benevolent light comes from a southern exposure. Eastern and western exposures offer less light, though there's still a long list of plants that can thrive with intermittent sun or partial shade, filtered through curtains. Northern exposure is the trickiest, and many people assume that nothing will grow successfully in this light, but that's not entirely true. The windows in my Manhattan apartment face north and east, and I've been able to grow several types of plants in almost total shade, among them clivia, scented geranium, African violet, and jade plant.

As invaluable as container plants are in bringing the

Right: *A primitive twig basket with a handle and pretty detailing keeps kitchen herbs—in this case, pots of parsley and chives—close at hand.*

A vignette reminiscent of the Provence region of France, where Lynn Chase found many of the pots and planters used on the deck, opposite. *A small lemon tree takes root in a large green glazed earthenware pot; stalks of 'Pacific Blue' delphinium provide textural and visual contrast to their terra-cotta container.*

Following pages: *A thirty-foot deck overlooking the Kennebunk River is where antiques dealer Lynn Chase has set his container garden. Three large terra-cotta columns—in reality, drainpipes—serve as a Romanesque backdrop for the foliage, from lemon trees to tomatillo plants.*

outdoors in, they can also enrich the outdoors itself. Large junipers and yews as well as various small pines or dogwoods can transform the terrace of a modern apartment building into an idyllic country scene. Seated amid the lush botanicals, you could almost forget you're in a metropolis, particularly if a few of the trees are strategically placed to obscure the view of the neighboring buildings. A terrace garden offers an expanse of greenery from inside an apartment as well: when you look out, the city recedes from sight and consciousness.

Even on a country terrace already surrounded by greenery, potted plants can have a dramatic impact. Given a lot of space, container gardening can be executed on a grand scale. Indeed, potted trees can grow quite large; in gardens in the Italian countryside it's not unusual to see potted olive or laurel trees that are a hundred years old. My friend Lynn Chase, a dealer in fine antiques, has an eclectic collection of over fifty containers on his deck in Maine. The containers are not only charming, they also have an ulterior purpose. Since the deck directly abuts the Kennebunk River, the pots act as a picturesque fence of flowers and foliage.

192

Garden Ornament

Ornamental objects give a garden character. In the same way that decorative details set the tone of a room, a single well-placed piece of statuary or a classic element, such as a sundial, can establish the mood of a garden. Decorative objects can also project a sense of history, giving a garden a timeless quality. Some of the most classic pieces are made of stone, which ages beautifully. There's something romantic about the look of stone as it slowly weathers, softening and graying. Terracotta is another inviting surface for moss, but while this earthenware holds up to inclement weather, it should be brought inside in winter to avoid cracking. Copper, however, is virtually indestructible; it reacts to the environment by turning an interesting shade of verdigris.

Page 196: *This well, constructed in the early 1930s, still functions. The terra-cotta capitals and roof tiles were brought from Italy and assembled on the site.*

Ornamentation on a grand scale, opposite: *an Italian marble fountain, set in formal gardens with a courtyard entrance.*

Formal symmetry, following pages: *The Hosmers' garden gate, which leads to lawns down by the sea, is flanked on either side by rounded boxwood hedges and stone columns topped by carved stone pineapple finials.*

A bronze sundial, about sixty years old, is set on a cast cement pedestal, pages 202–203. *It is topped by an astrolabe, an instrument that was replaced by the sextant in celestial navigation. The arrow is lined up with the equator.*

Not surprisingly, botanicals are a source of inspiration for garden ornament. One of the most popular motifs throughout the centuries has been the carved pineapple, which you see in all sorts of sizes and settings. The pineapple, a late-1800s symbol of welcome, became especially visible as garden ornamentation when sea captains, traveling back from the Azores or South America, began signaling their safe return by placing the exotic fruit on the picket of a fence post.

Fountains offer a more elaborate kind of ornamentation—one that's often quite dramatic. Formal or whimsical, Old World or contemporary, fountains are as natural to a garden setting as the proximity of a pond or lake. The sound of trickling water adds to the atmosphere—another element for the senses to take in.

Stone statuary can also transform a garden into a lyrical retreat. Statues, as well as stone benches, seats, and pedestals, have a romantic, European quality. What's more, they have a very substantial presence—a solidity and permanence—in contrast to the fragility and impermanence of plants.

An ornamental object serves yet another function: It gives a garden a structure, a focal point. A pair of copper urns can establish an entrance; a stone bench might mark a destination at the end of a path; a large birdbath set on a pedestal in the midst of a flower garden could define the center of the garden. The birdbath combines embellishment with function. It is not only lovely to look at; it also brings wildlife into the garden.

Even the most practical elements of a garden can have an ornamental impact. A fence or a wall defines the space and determines the look, both from a distance and from within the garden. A rough and irregular stone wall, in which each stone is handpicked to fit with the next, has pastoral charm and is reminiscent of the rambling English

and Irish countrysides. A picket fence, meanwhile, is very American in tradition and spirit and, when painted bright white, has a fresh kind of informality. A split-rail fence, more for definition than protection from animals, gives the most open feeling to a garden or property—it outlines the space without closing it off. The opposite, of course, is a tall wall—of hedges or stone—which gives the garden a feeling of complete privacy; when you're within its confines, you can't help but feel enclosed in a secret garden.

A garden gate is always an enticement to enter. It gives a garden the sense of a room to be explored; it beckons you to see what's beyond it. Gates run the gamut in style. A high, arched wrought-iron entranceway is formal and elegant, whereas a low, latched swinging gate is more casually welcoming—you feel as though you need no invitation to push it open and step inside.

Arbors can also act as an entrance to a garden, and they are probably the most enchanting of all doorways. An arbor can be fashioned from various materials—iron, wood, bamboo—but the real effect comes with the vines and climbing flowers (such as wisteria, honeysuckle, or clematis) that can

The decorative value of the apple, right: *Cornish gillyflower trees are espaliered against a stone fence and wooden door. Espaliered fruit trees are often a fixture in English and French gardens.*

Grapevines are used in an unusual, decorative way at the Hosmers': They are trained to climb over stable doors, opposite. *When the grapes—'Niagara,' 'Concord,' and 'Delaware' varieties—bear fruit in the fall, the vines look even more lovely and lush.*

A charming stone path, following pages: *Pieces of fieldstone placed in the grass form a decorative pattern and lead to a wide expanse of lawn and, in the distance, gardens.*

be trained to embellish the frame. Vines, in fact, can be trained to climb along almost any kind of architectural structure that allows them to twist and turn. They can also be coaxed to grow up the side or over a door with the help of a trellis or garden twine to hold the vine in place. In almost any guise, vines have a strong graphic presence; they become a dramatic piece of ornamentation.

206

Parties

Flower Arranging

The first summer I spent in Maine, I met some extraordinarily talented gardeners who dazzled me with their flower arrangements. One woman specialized in Japanese-style design, another had a flair for abstract and free-form creations. Perhaps the biggest influence of all was Marion Hosmer, who designed glorious arrangements from both flowers and vegetables grown in her extensive gardens. When I was asked to join the Piscataqua Garden Club as a summer guest, I immediately accepted. And I am so glad that I did. The experience altered any previous notion I had of what constitutes a flower arrangement.

One of the first things I learned is that "botanical" is a broad term that includes everything from flowers and twigs to leaves and fruit—and that these elements can be

213

A lovely greeting in a front hall, page 212: an airy arrangement of gloriosa lilies in a Venetian glass vase. When the flowers are as elaborate and exotic as these, they often look best when presented on their own.

A pantry sink, opposite, is ideal for cutting and arranging flowers, including rhododendron and mountain laurel. While waiting to be arranged in another vase, these blooms look charming in a French florist bucket.

Following pages: The strong yellow of the dining-room walls suggested the colors for this lively arrangement of yellow snap-dragons and white hydrangea. Placing the flowers in a low bowl ensures that guests can see one another over the top of the arrangement. A pair of decorative doves lends a pastoral air to the centerpiece.

A delicate arrangement on a bedside table, pages 218–219. Something as simple as a few stems of blue delphinium and white larkspur, cut to fit a small cut-crystal vase, makes a strong impression. The flowers echo the colors of the wallpaper —one of my prints, called Jacqueline.

mixed in any number of unorthodox ways. This concept is not new or avant-garde. In the seventeenth century the Flemish were the first to put fruits and flowers together, and they did so in a characteristically voluptuous manner that was captured in rich detail by painters of the period.

I also learned that flower arrangements can express something as intangible as mood. Often at our garden club meetings the assignment was to interpret a poem, a piece of music, or the concept of air or water—all through botanicals. We were taught to consider the entire composition, including the container (in garden club lexicon it's never called a vase). Even a decorative component, such as a lace doily or mat placed underneath the arrangement, adds to the total effect.

While the essence of flower arranging is personal interpretation, it helps to have a few guidelines. The most successful traditional arrangements have certain similarities that might escape the casual observer. There are three basic rules of thumb that have worked for me time and again:

- Height ratio: an arrangement at its highest point should be two-thirds taller than the height of the container. The lighter or airier the flowers, the higher the design may reach.
- An odd number of stems makes for a more interesting-looking arrangement; the extra flower adds a touch of unpredictability.
- Flowers with upright stems—such as daffodils, hyacinth, and day lilies—work better in a vase by themselves rather than mixed with other flowers. Their stems don't bend into graceful lines, so they are difficult to arrange.

Fragrance is another consideration when it comes to choosing flowers—and in placing arrangements in the home. Some blossoms have a heavenly scent, others next

to none, still others an unpleasant one. Among the most fragrant flowers are lily of the valley, lilacs, peonies, lilies, lavender, roses, tuberose, gardenias, honeysuckle, and hyacinth—any of which would make a welcome addition to a table in the front hall or by the bed. Potted plants, like scented geraniums or herbs such as rosemary, also give off a pleasant aroma.

Some of the most beautiful flowers, including iris, nasturtiums, poppies, foxglove, and clematis, have very little scent, which can be an advantage if you want to use them in a centerpiece on the dining-room table, they won't compete with the aromas of the meal.

Then there are those flowers that make up for a particularly pungent odor with their looks. Daisies, which have a quaint charm, also have an off-putting smell. Marigolds, which are little bursts of color, are a bit too piquant for some noses; these are blossoms best admired from a distance.

To many people, the most mystifying part of flower arranging is not the choosing of flowers per se but deciding on the container. Certainly one could argue that a delicate arrangement looks most natural in something small and refined, like a porcelain vase, while a casual bouquet of flowers is more suited to crockery. But uprooting tradition by placing pansies in a silver vase or fabulous country roses in a modern bubble vase is an equally valid and often more striking choice.

The container is, after all, half the look. Almost anything qualifies: demitasse cups, silver bowls, even baskets. Obviously, baskets aren't made for this purpose; you can adapt them by either placing a small glass inside or using a pinholder in a cup to hold water. Some of my favorite containers are from my collections. Majolica pitchers, for example, make picturesque vases—if they're not cracked. If they are, I do the same thing I do with a basket: simply

Vases of all varieties, opposite above: *Anything that can hold water can hold a flower, from a teacup to a teapot to a ceramic paper bag.*

Opposite below: *all the tools a flower arranger needs.* Clockwise, from upper right: *marbles, marble chips, wires of different gauges, wire cutters, a small hammer, clippers, wooden picks, florist's tape, large wire for wiring stems, plastic water picks, small perfume sample bottles, rings and pins to hold branches in place, a pen with indelible green ink, florist's clay, varieties of pinholders and pinholder chains, and glass and wire frogs. The wooden tray has holes and small dowels—the dowels can be secured around the completed arrangement so it can be easily transported. On the tray are small vases to hide extra stems in, an eyedropper for adding water to miniature arrangements, different types of picks, and miniature black pinholders.*

221

*A tiny arrangement with a lot of character,
right: 'Imperial Blue' pansies placed
in an antique English children's mug decorated with pansy-faced figures.*

*Opposite: This lush, casual arrangement—
'Miss Kim' and 'James McFarlane'
lilacs and 'Snow Mound' spirea—captures
the essence of summer. The height of the
arrangement—three and a half feet—fills
the visual space of the stairwell where
it is placed.*

*Fresh from the garden: a luscious bouquet
of 'Janet Blair' rhododendron in a
white ceramic tureen, following pages.*

place a small glass of water inside.

There is almost always a creative solution to a problem. While glass vases make lovely vessels for flowers, they offer a clear view of unsightly stems and leaves. The way around this is to fill the base of the vase with a camouflage of sorts: smooth black Japanese pebbles, a set of children's marbles, or for a festive holiday touch, fresh cranberries. (There's an added benefit to all these camouflages: They hold the flowers upright, acting almost as a pinholder.) To keep air bubbles at bay, I find it works well to boil the water first and then, once it has cooled, pour it into the glass vase— the result is flat, crystal-clear water.

Arrangements aside, many people are hesitant to invest in a constant supply of flowers; admittedly, the expense can be quite high. But flowers needn't cost the earth, not with so many greengrocers now selling tulips, narcissus, and stems of delphinium, along with the ubiquitous buckets of daisies. Garden centers also offer an increasingly esoteric selection of annuals and perennials for those who are interested in starting or enlarging their cutting garden.

If, however, you are going to choose expensive flowers, it makes sense to know which ones will live more than a

couple of days. Flowers that have a short-lived bloom often have clues in their names: day lilies last for just one day; morning glories are only out for a morning; and four-o'clocks peak in the late afternoon. At the other extreme are flowers that can live up to a week; zinnias, lilacs, and marigolds are three of the best-known types. As a general rule, arrange those flowers together that have similar life expectancies, so that half the arrangement doesn't droop while the other half is still standing tall. Nonetheless, if some flowers in an arrangement fade early, simply pull them out and rearrange the remaining flowers in a smaller container.

Before flowers are arranged in a container of any sort, they need conditioning. There's nothing more disappointing than to have roses droop an hour after you've placed them in a vase. To expedite the flow of water up the stem, flowers should be cut under cold running water as soon as you get them inside the house (the water prevents air bubbles from entering the stem and choking off the water supply). Use a sharp knife or clippers on an angle; the more angled the cut, the greater the intake of moisture. If the stem is woody, like a rose's, it's best to smash it with a hammer, which helps water get into the stem.

Even after the flowers are cut and in a vase, there are times they'll require a little tending. If flowers begin to wilt, it may be a simple matter of quenching thirst. To revive an arrangement, recut the stems and plunge the ends immediately into hot (not boiling) water, which moves into the stems faster than cold water. After about ten minutes, plunge the ends of the stems into cold water, then rearrange them in a vase of tepid water.

Much has been written about what can be added to the water to keep flowers and branches alive. I've found the following "recipes" work for particular flowers:

- Freesia can be revived with a solution of ½ teaspoon alcohol (gin or vodka) added to 1 quart warm water.
- Tulips stand straighter if a penny is dropped into the base of the container.
- Roadside flowers like Queen Anne's lace and goldenrod perk up when their stems are placed in a bucket filled with a mixture of 2 tablespoons dishwashing liquid to 1 quart water and stored in a cool, dark place overnight.
- Poppies and other milky-stemmed flowers like snow-on-the-mountain must be seared for about 40 seconds with a match or over a gas flame, then placed in water.
- Peonies can be incredibly fragile. To make them last

longer, cut their stems and split the ends. Let them stand for 2 to 3 hours in a solution of 1 quart water mixed with 3 tablespoons sugar. Never put peonies in Oasis—they are "allergic" to it.

Dried floral arrangements are not a substitute for live flowers, nor are they intended to be. They have their own kind of fragile, understated beauty. Certain flowers are better suited to the process. (Many flowers lose their looks when dried, turning an unattractive shade, or take on a strange scent.) Those that dry well include globe amaranth, hydrangea, lavender, roses and rosebuds, straw flowers, eucalyptus, and grapevines without leaves. Since the color of any blossom tends to darken as it dries, deep reds are not an ideal choice; colors in the light or medium range are most successful.

The mechanics of drying are straightforward—the simplest method is to empty out the water and allow the flowers to dry right in the vase. The other option, which helps the flowers retain their shape better, is to hang them upside down. In our country house, there are always flowers in various stages of dryness hanging from a rack in the kitchen. As a first step to drying, the flowers should be stripped of their leaves (which tend to shrivel unattractively); then the flowers should be hung in bunches spaced far enough apart that they won't compress one another and so that the air can circulate freely. The enemies of flower preservation are light and humidity, which is why attic rafters or even clotheslines hung in a spare closet are good locations.

There is a third, albeit more complicated, option for preserving flowers in a more "perfect" condition. The flower heads are carefully lowered into a jar filled with silica gel (available at nurseries or florists), so that they are covered. After several days, when the little dots in the gel have turned from blue to pink, the flowers are dry and can

be carefully removed with a slotted spoon. Once the gel is carefully dusted off with a sable watercolor brush, the flowers retain nearly all their original color and shape. It's also possible to use the gel over and over by drying it out in a warm oven until the dots turn blue again.

While dried arrangements can look quite dramatic or elegant, they can also look a bit, well, dry. The leaves and branches are brittle, so you don't get the sense of movement with a dry arrangement that you do with one made of fresh flowers. There are, however, some dried branches that are intrinsically graceful. Grapevines, corkscrew willow, and Harry Lauder's walking stick (a curly, twisted shrub) add a kinetic energy to any dried flower bouquet.

Potpourri is a variation of the dried flower arrangement. And while it's easy in theory (you simply dry flower petals and combine them in a bowl), what's trickier is to find a

230

A delicate bouquet of dried lavender, lily of the valley, and love-in-a-mist looks especially appropriate on a bedside table covered with a pullwork lace cloth, opposite above. A transferware platter and a lamp fashioned from an antique Chinese teapot complete the tableau.

An open-weave basket lined with Oasis holds a bouquet of grasses, opposite below: saffron, pampas grass, sea lavender, and local weeds and grasses.

A cabbage-leaf porcelain tureen, left, makes a perfect container for potpourri; the lid helps preserve the scent. The little bottle is filled with lavender essential oil, which helps refresh the fragrance as needed.

Following pages: Rhododendron and wild iris just clipped from the garden are placed in a homemade flower carrier.

pleasing balance of scents—the right ratio of petals to spices, of strong aromas to mild ones. There are recipes for potpourri, but it's really more a matter of trial and error, a pinch of this or that. I often use lavender as my base; in the bleakness of winter the fragrance fills me with thoughts of gardening. Some of my favorite ingredients to add to the lavender are bay leaves, rosemary, cinnamon, cloves, and orange, lemon, or tangerine peel.

I combine the botanical ingredients together in a glass or pottery bowl (which won't absorb odors the way wood will), and using a small dropper, add several drops of an essential oil (such as lavender, rose geranium, jasmine, or lemon verbena). I then store the mix in a jar with a tight-fitting lid, stirring every so often, until one fragrance seems to meld into another—which takes about a week or two.

Once "cured," the potpourri can either be sewn into sachets or set into bowls, in which case I like to pile the petals high so the colors really show. If the scent starts to trail off after a few weeks, you can add a few drops of an essential oil and crunch the potpourri petals between your fingers to reactivate the spices and herbs. The fragrance will once again fill the air.

MORNING GLORY HOUSE POTPOURRI

Many of the ingredients in my favorite potpourri are simple kitchen staples.

4 ounces whole cloves
6 ounces dried lavender flowers
2 ounces dried orange peel, cut into 2-inch strips
1 ounce ground allspice
1 ounce ground cinnamon
2 ounces whole bay leaves
1 ounce powdered orrisroot (optional)
10 to 12 drops lavender oil
2 ounces blue delphinium flower heads

Mix all the ingredients except the delphinium in a glass bowl. Cover with plastic wrap and let sit for two weeks while the scents blend, stirring every two days. Place in a ceramic or porcelain bowl, then add the delphinium at the very end for decoration and color—the delphinium flowers crush easily, so it's best not to stir them.

The Indoor Party

Designing a table setting is not unlike painting a still life. It's a matter of composition, of arranging the elements—linens, flowers, china, silver—to form a striking tableau. But it is also more. I find that what separates the memorable table from the mundane is the presence of a unifying theme, whether overt or subtle. That theme can be inspired by the color of a set of plates or by their country of origin. Sometimes I find ideas for a table setting in a botanical detail: the garlands on a porcelain vase, the sculptured rosebud handle of a silver spoon, the radish embroidered on the edge of a napkin. As in nature, the variations are endless, and so are the possibilities for creating table settings with a botanical leitmotif.

A botanical panoply, page 236: *The antique German china is hand-painted with cartouches of flowers; an ecru place mat has delicate cutwork florals; and the damask linen napkin displays a pansy pattern.*

Floral motifs often grace silver, particularly antique pieces, giving them a sculptural quality and a more decorative presence. This unusual set, opposite, *a gift from my mother, has raised clusters of grapes and vines.*

Following pages: *The use of good silverware and linens gives breakfast the feel of an out-of-the-ordinary occasion. In my New York apartment, a white cotton tablecloth with a pretty fagoted border is topped by a smaller periwinkle-blue French jacquard cloth. A jacquard napkin also lines a basket of jams, for a country touch. The fruit is a treat as well: gooseberries in handle-less teacups and 'Princess Anne' cherries on a small platter.*

To set the tone for a country-style breakfast in my city apartment, I used cheerful blue-and-white pottery decorated with bucolic scenes. While the plates and cups are quite delicate, what keeps the table from feeling overly formal is the mix; I chose a variety of transferware pieces with different patterns and pastoral designs. The shared color scheme (white backgrounds with blue designs in a range of hues) unifies the disparate elements, giving the table a pleasantly eclectic look.

Linens of blue and white, the quintessential country color scheme, are in keeping with the style of the pottery. Layering the linens—a white cotton tablecloth topped by a periwinkle-blue jacquard cloth and napkins—adds to the table's cozy feel.

The use of pretty pottery and linens—even with a breakfast as simple as fresh fruit, muffins, and jams—is a treat. Most people don't bother making a fuss over breakfast, nor do they expect it. But if you have the time, a sit-down breakfast at an elegantly set table is a wonderful break from routine; it can make you feel as if you're on holiday.

White asparagus, opposite, *is a cousin of the more familiar green variety. Similar in taste, it is grown in a sheltered environment so that photosynthesis never takes place. The pitcher is a wild-rose-and-butterfly majolica pattern. The silver serving pieces are embossed with roses, leaves, and scrolls.*

Botanical motifs give a lunch for two a country feel, following pages: *The curtains are antique crewelwork; the ivy-patterned rug is from my collection for New River Artisans; the pillows on the chairs are made from a toile de Jouy similar to that of the place mats; and the eyelet tablecloth is embroidered with delicate flowers.*

This asparagus plate, pages 246–247, *found in Paris, has a fanciful quality. The printed napkin has a faience pattern; and a toile de Jouy place mat depicts French maidens in a garden vignette.*

A vegetable of a much different kind, the white asparagus, was the inspiration for a Provençal-style luncheon in the library of my Manhattan apartment. I first became aware of white asparagus during a trip to Paris in the late 1970s, when I bought a colorful majolica plate decorated with the embossed image of the vegetable. I thought that white asparagus was only an artist's dream until I learned that it really does exist. In Europe white asparagus is grown in early spring through the miracle of engineered gardening. I promised myself that should I ever return to Paris, I would try to find another plate. Thirteen trips later, I have a collection of thirteen.

The naive quality of the majolica pottery gave this luncheon a lighthearted air. Each of the unique hand-painted plates has a different design of asparagus spears and a different brilliantly colored background. Once again, the pottery influenced the menu, which featured white asparagus itself, bought from a specialty produce market.

To add to the French theme, I used place mats fashioned from pieces of antique toile de Jouy (French linen printed with pastoral scenes), which I found in the Marché aux Puces flea market on the outskirts of Paris. Even if the guests were unaware of the fabric's origin, I knew. For me, this detail made the table setting complete.

Opposite: *The Oriental origins of the china inspired the luncheon's main course of steamed shrimp with dillweed. Small export bowls hold various garnishes and fruits and vegetables. On the sideboard in the background, two large export vases holding eucalyptus leaves flank an export tea service. On the windowsill, a silver epergne holds roses and tuberose. The desserts on the small side table include petits fours decorated with candied violets, rose petals, and yellow sugar-coated mimosa seeds found in an Oriental gourmet food shop.*

Not your usual centerpiece, following pages: *Two rare export cachepots on rosewood lacquered stands hold bunches of radishes (three each). The radishes were sprayed with a mist of vegetable oil to give them a slight sheen; otherwise they would look dusty and dry.*

For a sit-down luncheon in the dining room of my apartment, the formal sensibility was established with a collection of old export china, the term for the hand-painted china exported from China to Europe and other destinations starting in the eighteenth century. Each of the delicate plates has a different pastel flower design, yet all share a celadon background, giving the table a cohesive appearance.

I am a great believer in using valuable pieces in a practical way, even if it means taking them off the wall or shelf where they are displayed. As beautiful as a plate is, it was made to be used. Entertaining friends is occasion and reason enough.

The Venetian linens for this luncheon inspired another theme for the setting. The place mats and napkins are delicately embroidered with a variety of fruits, vegetables, and whimsical beetles—and in each corner, a lovely little radish. From there came the idea for the centerpiece: two export cachepots filled with radishes turned upside down so their roots show. While not a typical centerpiece element, the radish has a striking red color, and when many are grouped together they have a strong sculptural presence. I've learned that in order to set an original table you have to be willing to take something out of its expected context, to look at it from a fresh angle. Even a root vegetable can have beauty.

When it comes to the most formal of tables, I believe there should be a consideration of structure and of symmetry. The less crowded the table, the more the china, silver, and stemware can be appreciated.

In setting the table for this dinner party for six, I decided to use lace place mats rather than a tablecloth. The hard edges of the mahogany table made the setting a bit more formal than it would have been had the table been covered by a soft cloth. The wood surface reflected the glow of the candles, while the gold trim on the china and stemware added a glimmer of their own.

To me the finishing touch of a formal table is the centerpiece. It's the first thing guests notice as they approach the table. As grand as you make it, however, guests should still be able to look over the centerpiece when they're seated, which usually means the flowers should be no more than ten inches above the table height or, alternatively, they should be staggered between place settings so guests can see each other through them.

There is really no strict definition of what a centerpiece is or should be. In fact, a centerpiece is saddled with a bit of an image problem. Many people think of it as contrived and staid, but it can also be quite inventive and original. Perhaps the term "centerpiece" is too limiting and the arrangement should be called something entirely different—a "table landscape" or "tablepiece."

Arrangements aside, I often like to add a more intimate decorative touch to the table. My personal signature for a formal dinner party is a treat for each guest, a sophisticated party favor, such as unusual white asparagus chocolates tied with a gold bow. This kind of favor never fails to elicit surprise and delight.

The Outdoor Party

*D*ining in the open air is a sensual, often exhilarating experience. It also expands the possibilities for inventive parties; you can draw on your surroundings for inspiration as well as decorative effect. The flowers or vegetables from a nearby garden, for instance, might be used on the table as a centerpiece or as part of the menu itself.

While most people think of an outdoor party as a casual meal on the deck or, at the other extreme, a wedding under a tent, there's a world of options in between, from a luncheon in the middle of a vegetable garden to a lobster supper by the sea. Regardless of the venue or the formality of the event, my approach to entertaining is no different out of doors than it is indoors. I take the same care in setting the

The makings for a Fourth of July buffet, page 256. *The dinner plates are old English and French blue-and-white pottery; the blue-and-white napkins are made from my Seaweed fabric pattern; the balloonflowers on the left are in a ginger jar; and the bachelor's buttons are in an English teapot.*

The luxury of breakfast in a glorious garden overlooking the Atlantic Ocean, following pages. *The table is set in a clearing by a bed of soft lemon-yellow day lilies, called 'Hyperion,' which bloom from mid-June to late July. The chintz tablecloth has a pattern of sea fans, or, as I call them, flowers of the sea, from my Pretty Rooms Collection of fabrics and wallpapers. For comfort, not to mention style, I tied a cushion made of the same material as the tablecloth onto the seats.*

table, I give the same attention to detail, and I believe in using good-quality tableware—china, silver, and linens. There isn't any reason, other than inclement weather, that an outdoor party can't be sophisticated and original.

The first meal of the day is a chance to entertain on a small scale in a grand way. Even when the food is kept quite simple, you can make an occasion out of the meal by setting the table with style.

For a breakfast at our house in Maine, I chose a spot in my perennial garden of day lilies and flowering herbs overlooking the Atlantic Ocean. To give the meal a special cachet, a small round wooden table was brought out to the edge of the garden and covered with a chintz table skirt. With a generous enough cloth you can provide a pretty camouflage for any kind of table, even a card table. The table was set with a very lovely English pottery from the early 1900s known as calyxware (calyx is actually a term for botanical ornamentation). I also brought out a pair of old country maple chairs, which, in their new context, looked quite elegant.

Once I decided to serve the breakfast by the bed of day lilies, I didn't have to look far for decorative inspiration. I used the lily itself as part of the meal—as a cornucopia for raspberries. Not only do the lilies look exquisite, they're edible! The profusion of color on the table and off, along with the smell of the earth and flowers, made for an intoxicating way to start the day.

Baskets brim with colorful vegetables and fruits, opposite: radicchio, broccoli, cauliflower, artichokes, and purple cabbages in one; grapes and nectarines in another; and perfect garden tomatoes in a third. Antique grain shovels are used to serve a mix of cheeses.

Following pages: A "formal" picnic is set up in a clearing near a vegetable garden in Maine. In the spirit of a traditional picnic, the tablecloth is classic red and white. Instead of the typical checkered pattern, however, the cloth has a botanical motif of Chinese chrysanthemums. The red-and-white linens lining various baskets on the buffet table are actually vintage dish towels; all they needed was a good washing and little spray starch to make them crisp.

A fiesta of color blooms in the vegetable garden of my friend Lynn Eaton, who lives year-round in Maine. Her well-planned and bountiful garden—with zucchini, tomatoes, onions, and eggplant—provided an unique site for a box lunch picnic. It's a treat to be in the middle of a garden surrounded by vegetables, and at the same time to be able to enjoy those same vegetables as part of the meal.

As charming as unusual settings can be, however, they sometimes present practical challenges. In this case, there was the problem of the ground, not the most ideal of floorings. The solution was a mulch of salt-marsh hay that was laid down over it. The earth became a soft, pleasant surface—more even, too, so that balancing a dining-room table became easy.

Part of the pleasure in giving a party that's distinctive in some way is looking for creative ways to present the food. Lynn happens to be a collector of antique kitchenware, and a quick tour of her kitchen yielded utensils that could be turned into charming ad hoc serving pieces. I used her antique grain shovels as cheese platters, and an old wooden drawer divider (originally designed for silverware) as a container for a pretty mix of dried fruits. As for the box part of the lunch, I bought small cookie boxes from a local baker and packed a sandwich, fruit, bread, cheese, and sparkling water—the idea being that guests could wander from the buffet table, lunch in hand, to explore the gardens and the neighboring woods.

LEMON CURD TARTLETS

My friend Becky Linney makes the most wonderful small lemon curd tarts—sweet with a citrus tang. I like to embellish them with a thin wedge of lime or lemon peel or a few berries from the garden, along with a sprinkling of confectioners' sugar.

1½ cups sugar
¼ cup cornstarch
¼ teaspoon salt
½ cup unsalted butter, cut into small pieces
1½ cups boiling water
3 egg yolks
1 whole egg
Juice and grated zest of 2 medium lemons
Double batch of Pie Pastry, baked as tartlet shells (page 287)
Fresh raspberries, blueberries, thin wedges of lemon and lime, and confectioners' sugar, for garnish

Sift the sugar, cornstarch, and salt together into the top of a double boiler.

In a bowl, blend the butter and boiling water until the butter melts, then add to the dry ingredients in the double boiler. Mix. Beat the egg yolks and the whole egg together, then slowly whisk into the sugar-butter mixture.

Cook over simmering water, constantly stirring, until the mixture thickens (or until the mixture coats the back of a spoon). Remove from heat, add lemon juice and zest, mix well, and set aside to cool for about 1 hour.

Pour into the cooled baked tartlet shells. Refrigerate the tartlets for at least an hour before serving. Garnish with raspberries, blueberries, lemon wedges, lime wedges, and a sprinkling of confectioners' sugar.

Makes 24 to 28 tartlets.

There's arguably no more idyllic site for a picnic than the bluffs of Maine's craggy coast. In such a majestic setting, even a simple picnic can have a sophisticated air. To give the meal a stylish basis, I laid down an antique quilt. As long as a quilt isn't too delicate, there's no reason not to bring it out of the house. In fact, a quilt is better suited to a picnic than the standard checkered cloth because it provides a more substantial "tabletop." In another effort to elevate the picnic beyond the ordinary, I used ceramic plates instead of paper. Ceramic plates are not only an aesthetic consideration but a thoughtful and pragmatic one: They're easier to balance on the lap than paper. It may seem a burden to carry all this equipment to a picnic site, but for the difference it makes, it is well worth any extra effort.

For me every table setting—even one in such an informal environment—deserves flowers. I took along unbreakable old silverplate teapots to use as vases and collected greens and berries from the site. Once the impromptu arrangements were placed on the quilt, the table was set, so to speak.

SCOTCH SHORTBREAD WITH JOHNNY-JUMP-UPS

These shortbread cookies are rich and buttery. Dabbed with a little icing and decorated with a Johnny-jump-up from the garden, they become something rather special.

1 cup unsalted butter, softened
½ cup sugar
2 cups flour

Preheat the oven to 325 degrees.

Cream the butter well. Add the sugar and beat until light and fluffy. Gradually add the flour, blending well. Pat evenly and firmly into the bottom of an 8 × 12-inch baking dish. Bake for 20 to 25 minutes, until evenly puffed and just starting to brown around the edges. Be careful not to overbake. Remove from the oven and cut immediately into bite-size squares. Set the pan on a rack to cool. Remove the squares and frost.

Makes 32 squares.

FROSTING

1 cup confectioners' sugar
1 tablespoon unsalted butter, softened
½ teaspoon vanilla extract
2 to 3 teaspoons milk
1 or 2 drops green food coloring (optional)
Johnny-jump-ups, for garnish

Combine the confectioners' sugar, butter, and vanilla in a bowl. Add the milk, a little at a time, beating well. Add only enough milk to give an easy spreading consistency—the icing should be as firm as possible. Blend in a few drops of green food coloring, if desired. Frost shortbread squares and top each with a single Johnny-jump-up.

Makes 1 cup.

Shortbread cookies topped with flowers called Johnny-jump-ups pick up the yellow of the colorful quilt on the ground and the octagonal plate, above.

Following pages: What makes this picnic *unique is both the food (soup, biscuits, cherry tomatoes, shortbread cookies) and the table setting (an antique quilt in the Lone Star pattern, basketry, and china). The purple cabbages make a vividly colorful centerpiece.*

269

The ivy leaf as decorative motif, above: *a delicate wrought-iron garden chair from the late 1930s.*

The ivy theme is reiterated throughout the setting, opposite: *A sprig of ivy is used as a napkin ring, tying the silverware at each plate; the napkin is green-and-white linen; the green luncheon plate is an old Wedgwood pattern; the butter-pat plate is a transferware pattern; the pressed goblets are from the late nineteenth century and have ivy detail. The nasturtium flowers—adding a dash of color—are laid over a bed of ruffled Romaine lettuce. The petals taste as good as they look and, served on a platter rather than in a bowl, are displayed to advantage.*

The more formal a luncheon the more important it is to have a theme; it helps to give the table unity and polish. This luncheon for six, served at the edge of a perennial garden bordering a cornfield in Maine, was designed around the motif of the ivy plant. (Ivy, one of the most formal types of foliage, also happens to be quite easy to grow—inside in a window box or outside as a ground cover.) For this party I mixed the real with the decorative: The plant appears in a centerpiece and as sculptural leaves on wrought-iron chairs.

The ivy plant also inspired the color scheme of green and white. The greens used here are not a strict match, yet like a garden full of various shades of color—some greens with more yellow or blue or gray in them—the overall look is harmonious. In the midst of all the green, a salad of vibrantly colored nasturtiums, which were in full bloom in the garden, added a splash of contrast.

272

NASTURTIUM FLOWER AND LEAF SALAD

3 large handfuls of nasturtium leaves
18 nasturtium flowers
2 small heads Bibb or Boston lettuce
½ cup Garlic Vinaigrette

Carefully wash the nasturtium and lettuce leaves and flowers, being careful not to bruise them. Let them air-dry on paper towels and keep refrigerated until serving.

Tear the lettuce into pieces and combine with the nasturtium leaves after tossing in a bowl. Toss the salad gently with dressing. Garnish with the nasturtium flowers.

Makes 6 lunch-size servings.

DRESSING

6 tablespoons olive oil
1 tablespoon cider vinegar
1 tablespoon lemon juice
1 small garlic clove, minced
½ teaspoon French mustard
Salt and pepper to taste

Combine all ingredients in a bowl and beat with a wire whisk until thoroughly blended. Store any leftover dressing in a jar in the fridge.

Makes ½ cup.

LEMON GERANIUM LEAF POUND CAKE

2¼ cups cake flour (not self-rising)
¼ teaspoon salt
2 teaspoons baking powder
1 cup unsalted butter, softened
1 cup sugar
4 eggs
1 teaspoon vanilla extract
1 tablespoon poppy seeds
¼ cup chopped lemon geranium leaves

Preheat the oven to 325 degrees.

Sift the flour into a small bowl, then resift, adding the salt and baking powder.

In the large bowl of an electric mixer, cream the butter. Gradually beat the sugar into the butter during 5 minutes of beating. Add the eggs, one at a time, during an additional 3 minutes of beating. Beat in the vanilla and poppy seeds. Gradually add the flour mixture, beating at low speed only until blended. Fold in geranium leaves.

Pour the batter into 2 greased and floured 6-cup baby fluted tube pans or 2 greased and floured 8½ × 4½ × 2¾-inch loaf pans, smoothing the tops.

Bake for 35 to 40 minutes, or until the top of cake is golden brown and a cake tester or toothpick inserted in center comes out clean. Cool in pans set on racks for 10 minutes. Remove from pans and cool completely on racks.

Serves 12 to 16.

Mixed greens, preceding pages: a 1940s tablecloth with a green border of leaves and flowers; green wrought-iron chairs, their seats covered with ivy-patterned fabric (Ivy from my Romance collection of fabrics and wallpapers); green-and-white transferware pottery; and the ivy plant itself as centerpiece. In the background: the perennial garden of lilium, coreopsis, foxglove, daisies, and bluebells, to name a few.

All colors of nasturtium are equally delectable—yellow, cream, orange, and maroon can be mixed together, opposite above. The smaller the leaves and flowers, however, the more delicate they are, so select carefully.

Opposite below: the icing on the cake— flowers that not only are an exquisite burst of color but can also be eaten along with the cake itself, a Lemon Geranium Leaf Pound Cake. Scented geranium leaves are added for their aroma (in this case lemon, though there are many types of scented geraniums) and nasturtium leaves for their delicate peppery bite.

These tea sandwiches, right, were cut into flower shapes with a small cookie cutter and garnished with flowering heads and leaves of herbs (dill, summer savory, marjoram, and mint). The silver tray is decorated with a grape-and-trellis motif.

Opposite: A Victorian silver vase holds an assortment of roses in pale pink and almost-ivory. The Coalport tea service with hand-painted rosebuds dates from the early 1800s.

Tea with great style in the Hosmers' perennial garden in Maine, following pages. *Lace and linens cover the two tables. A Victorian cotton parasol embroidered with white flowers leans against one of the cane-and-mahogany chairs. The tiered dessert stand holds petits fours decorated with candied violets and ginger cookies topped with fresh 'Red Lake' currants. Tea sandwiches are presented on a silver platter. An oval lattice porcelain "basket" is filled with lemon drops.*

HERB TEA SANDWICHES

1 loaf sliced soft white bread
2 tablespoons butter, softened
3 ounces spreadable cheese, such as cream cheese or goat cheese, softened
Assorted herb heads and flowers, including dill, marjoram, tarragon, mint, and rosemary

Cut the bread into flower shapes using a 2- or 3-inch cookie cutter. (You can save the trimmings for bread crumbs.) Lightly butter the bread, then spread with 1 teaspoon cheese and garnish with an herb head or flower.

Makes 18 to 24 sandwiches.

An afternoon tea in a flower garden is a glorious way to spend an hour or two, particularly when the garden is as breathtaking as the well-established perennial garden at the home of Marion Hosmer. In the late afternoon, with the golden light dappling the table, the scene is enchanting.

Part fantasy, part luxury, a tea party is an opportunity to indulge in decorative flourishes that under other circumstances might seem overwrought. For this particular tea, a round table was covered with an antique lace table skirt and topped with doilies, giving the table a timeless elegance. All the linens used were in varying shades of white, which made a particularly striking contrast to the deep greens and bright colors of the flower garden.

Floral motifs are a natural theme for a tea party set in a garden, and I used them unabashedly. They appeared in the tea service that was hand-painted with roses, and in a tiny silver vase embossed with a daisy. Flowers even adorned the food itself. As long as the floral decoration is light-handed, there's no such thing as too much.

Sun . . . beach . . . lobster. To me those three words tell the story of summer. Every July at our home in Maine we host a lobster dinner for neighbors and friends, sometimes as an Independence Day celebration. The setting is the back lawn, bordered by a perennial flower garden, with the ocean visible and audible in the distance.

In fact, it was the ocean that inspired the party's color scheme. Blue and white, a crisp combination, was the perfect foil for the dramatic red of the lobsters and the yellow of the corn. A formal white linen tablecloth was laid over an ordinary picnic table, giving the table the look of a proper buffet (a strategically placed stone under a wobby leg can help with balance, if necessary).

The table was then set with a variety of old English and French blue-and-white dinnerware, and embellished with floral arrangements in shades of blue. Here I used balloonflowers and bachelor's buttons from my cutting garden. (Blue flowers are not particularly common in nature, which makes them stand out.) For another blue still life I placed a small creamer holding blueberries in various stages of ripeness; a pretty addition to the table and a salute to summer's bounty.

CUCUMBER HORS D'OEUVRES

3 ounces spreadable cheese
2 cucumbers, washed but unpeeled,
sliced ¼-inch thick
Assorted herb heads and flowers, including dill, marjoram, tarragon,
mint, and rosemary

Spread a thin layer of cheese over each slice of cucumber and garnish with an herb head or flower.

Makes 56 hors d'oeuvres.

BECKY LINNEY'S BLACKBERRY PIE

This dessert brings with it memories of summer. To enjoy the berry flavor year round, substitute 20 ounces frozen blackberries, thawed, with their juice.

1½ cups sugar
¼ cup flour
½ teaspoon ground cinnamon
¼ teaspoon ground nutmeg
⅛ teaspoon salt
3 tablespoons quick-cooking tapioca
4 cups fresh blackberries, washed,
drained, and picked over
Pie Pastry for lattice-top pie
(recipe follows)
Juice of 1 lime
1 tablespoon unsalted butter, cut
into small pieces
Milk and sugar, for glaze

Preheat the oven to 425 degrees.

Sift the sugar, flour, cinnamon, nut-meg, and salt together. Stir in the tap-ioca. Mix in the berries. Pour into a 9-inch pastry-lined pie pan (bottom crust should be oversized). Sprinkle the lime juice over the berries and dot with butter. Weave strips of the remaining pastry in a lattice pattern over the top, pressing the ends into the edge of the bottom crust. Fold the bottom crust up, trimming if necessary, and press to se-cure. Flute the edges, then brush the strips lightly with milk and sprinkle with additional sugar.

Bake for 10 minutes, reduce the heat to 350 degrees and bake for an ad-ditional 40 to 55 minutes, or until the filling is bubbling near the center and the crust is nicely browned. Let cool, and serve at room temperature.

Serves 6.

PIE PASTRY

2 cups flour
½ teaspoon salt
⅔ cup cold shortening
5 tablespoons ice water

Sift the flour and salt together into a medium bowl. Cut in the shortening with a pastry blender until the pieces are the size of small peas. Sprinkle the ice water, a tablespoon at a time, over the mixture, blending gently with pas-try blender until all is moistened. Form the dough into a ball, wrap in plastic wrap, and chill for about half an hour.

For lattice-top Blackberry Pie: Roll out ⅔ of pastry on a floured board. Fit into a 9-inch pie pan. Roll out the remaining pastry and cut into ½-inch strips for the lattice top. Bake according to pie recipe.

For Lemon Curd Tartlets: Preheat the oven to 375 degrees. Roll out half the pastry at a time. Cut to fit shallow 3-inch round tartlet pans or 4-inch-long barquette molds. Press the dough into the pans, trim edges, and prick all over with a fork. Place the pans on a baking sheet and line with 4-inch squares of foil. Fill with dried beans or pie weights. Bake for 12 to 15 minutes. Re-move the foil and beans and return the tartlet shells to the oven for 5 to 10 min-utes, until lightly browned. Cool on a rack. Carefully remove the tartlet shells from pans when cool. (Make 2 batches of pastry to use up all of the lemon filling.)

A tiered tray made of wrought iron and bought at a general store in Maine holds finger food, opposite above: cucum-bers topped with cream cheese, herbs, and purple broccoli florets; and steamed snow peas.

Opposite below: The quintessential country dessert, blackberry pie, is made more so with botanical decoration. My friend Becky Linney made this lattice-crust pie with wild local blackberries and then encircled the edge with crystallized mint leaves. A vine of blackberries embellishes the stoneware platter, embossed with sheaves of wheat. The silver pie server has an all-over floral pattern.